# Predators

Written by Steve Parker
Designed by Jo Ryan

priddy books

# what is a predator?

Predators are animals that hunt and kill other creatures for food. They have extra-special senses, such as brilliant eyesight or amazing hearing, to find their victims.

**Big-eared bat**
Large, hear-all ears

**Lioness**
Long, pointed teeth

They have deadly weapons, like sharp claws and pointed teeth, which they use to catch and kill.

**Owl**

See-all eyes

Predators come in all shapes and sizes, from massive killer whales and cunning tigers, to slinky snakes and sneaky spiders. However, they all have one thing in common. They would rather tear up and gobble down their victims, known as prey, than munch on plants!

**Bear**

Super-smell nose

Each predator score shows how successful they are as hunters!

💀💀💀💀💀 Will attack, but not always successfully

💀💀💀💀💀 Will attack and cause injury

💀💀💀💀💀 Will attack, causing injury or death

💀💀💀💀💀 Most attacks prove fatal

💀💀💀💀💀 This predator is deadly

To help you imagine how big they are, you can compare their sizes to an adult. For smaller predators we use an adult hand instead.

Found in warm waters, great whites are most people's idea of a 'killer' shark. They are large, fearsome predators, and although they have attacked people, a great white would much rather eat a seal or sea lion! This shark's teeth are razor-sharp, jagged, and arranged in rows. As with all sharks, when a tooth breaks off, another one moves into its place.

Rows of razor-sharp teeth

# Great White Shark

**Predator score**

**Size up to:**
20 ft (6 m)
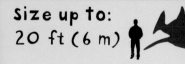

**Top speed:**
25 mph (40 km/h)

**HOW DANGEROUS?**
☠ ☠ ☠ ☠ ☠

# Cheetah

Its spotted coat allows it to hide easily out on the African grasslands

## Killer fact

A cheetah is so quick, it can accelerate to 60 mph (97 km/h) in just three seconds!

The cheetah is the fastest animal on land, able to run at a top speed of 75 mph (120 km/h). It eats small rabbits and birds, as well as larger animals such as springboks and gazelles. In a group, cheetahs even hunt wildebeests and zebras.

### Predator score

Size up to:
5 ft (1.5 m)

Top Speed:
75 mph (120 km/h)

HOW DANGEROUS?
☠ ☠ ☠ ☠ ☠

# Black Mamba

Its tongue and mouth are black

This African snake **slithers** faster than you can **run.** It can also climb trees and **swim** like a fish! When it catches a victim, like a rat or bird, it bites with its two long front fangs. These inject **deadly** venom, the prey dies, and the mamba **swallows** it in one go!

## Predator score

Size up tp:
14 ft (4.5 m)
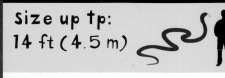

Top speed:
12 mph (20 km/h)

HOW DANGEROUS?

# Polar Bear

White coat provides camouflage in the Arctic snow and ice

**Killer fact**
Polar bears will swim up to 100 miles (161 km) at a time in search of their next kill.

The polar bear is one of the world's largest land predators. Its **powerful** body and huge feet break through thick ice to catch its favourite meal of seals. White fur means it can creep close to unsuspecting prey, or wait unnoticed at the seal's breathing hole in the ice.

## Predator score

Size up to:
10 ft (3 m)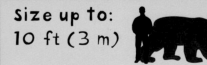

Top Speed:
25 mph (40 km/h)

They'll feed on anything they can get their jaws on

# Crocodile

**Killer fact**
Crocodiles have the strongest bite of any animal on Earth, easily able to bite through bone!

Crocodiles are large, heavy reptiles with very powerful jaws full of sharp, cone-shaped teeth. They wait quietly in shallow water for large animals to come and drink, then they snatch them in their mouths and pull them into the water to drown.

**Predator score**

Size up to:
20 ft (6 m)

Top Speed:
11 mph (18 km/h)

HOW DANGEROUS?

# Tiger

Tigers creep close enough to attack unsuspecting prey

The tiger is the **largest** of the big cats, and lives in the rainforests, mountains and grasslands of parts of Asia and Russia. Tigers can **leap** distances of 33 feet (10 m). They kill buffalo five times their size, by locking their huge jaws around the buffalo's **neck**, so it cannot breathe.

## Predator score

**Size up to:**
6 ft (1.8 m)

**Top Speed:**
40 mph (64 km/h)

**HOW DANGEROUS?**

# African Fish Eagle

**Killer fact**
African fish eagles sometimes catch monkeys, flamingos, and even small crocodiles!

Eagles are **large** birds of prey with strong **beaks** and long, sharp claws. They have excellent **eyesight,** which they use to spot their prey before swooping down to catch it. The African fish eagle is one of the largest eagles, with a huge **wingspan** of up to 8 feet (2.4 m).

Their sharp claws are called talons

**Predator score**

Size up to:
30 in (76 cm)

Top speed:
60 mph (97 km/h)

HOW DANGEROUS?

# Killer Whale

## Killer fact
Also called orcas, killer whales are brave enough to attack sharks, even great whites!

Killer whales work together to create waves that knock seals off of the sea ice

Killer whales often hunt and feed in groups called **pods**. This means they can attack much **bigger** prey than one killer could catch on its own — even an **enormous** whale. These **speedy** swimmers also eat fish, squid, seals, and seabirds such as albatrosses and penguins, throughout the oceans.

## Predator score
**Size up to:**
32 ft (9.8 m)

**Top speed:**
30 mph (48 km/h)

**HOW DANGEROUS?**
☠ ☠ ☠ ☠ ☠

In the rivers, lakes, and swamps of South America, one piranha may not seem very fierce, but when a whole shoal of piranhas smell blood, they seem to go crazy. They attack almost anything that moves with hundreds of sets of razor-sharp teeth in fast-snapping jaws.

Mouth full of flesh-tearing teeth

# Piranha

**Predator score**

| Size up to: |
| --- |
| 12 in (30 cm) |

| Top Speed: |
| --- |
| 15 mph (24 km/h) |

HOW DANGEROUS?

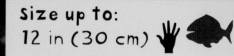

Their excellent hearing is good enough to hear a leaf falling onto the ground

Wolves can survive on fruits and other plants if needed, but they love to eat meat and hunt. A lone wolf catches small prey, such as rabbits and birds. A whole pack can bring down really big victims like deer and wild cows in the remote parts of North America, Asia, and Europe.

## Grey Wolf

### Predator score

Size up to:
5 ft (1.6 m)

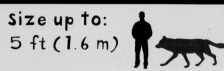

Top Speed:
40 mph (64 km/h)

HOW DANGEROUS?

Mainly found in Africa, this sleek animal is sudden **death** to lizards, frogs, birds, or big bugs. This furry hunter attacks like lightning with sharp claws and teeth. It is small, **bendy,** and short-legged enough to follow rats down into their burrows.

## Killer fact

The mongoose kills deadly snakes using fast reactions. Its thick fur protects against the snake's bite.

They move quickly and with great agility on their feet

# Mongoose

## Predator score

**Size up to:**
25 in (64 cm)

**Top speed:**
15 mph (24 km/h)

**HOW DANGEROUS?**

☠ ☠ ☠ ☠ ☠

# Grizzly Bear

If the grizzly has to, it can **survive** on fruits, berries, and wild bees' honey, but it is big and strong enough to prey on deer, wild sheep, and goats. In the autumn it loves to hook big fish from rivers using its curved claws.

## Killer fact

## Predator score

**Size up to:**
8 ft (2.4 m)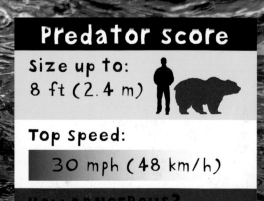

**Top speed:**
30 mph (48 km/h)

**HOW DANGEROUS?**
☠ ☠ ☠ ☠ ☠

Grizzlies go crazy for salmon, tearing it apart

Its tough body helps it survive the cold north as it searches for its next meal

The size of an average pet dog, the wolverine is a truly **powerful** and ferocious predator. It can bring down deer many times its own size. It lives in remote northern lands, here any prey has to be attacked fast — another meal may not come along for many days.

# Wolverine

## Predator score

**Size up to:**
4 ft (1.1 m)

**Top speed:**
30 mph (48 km/h)

**HOW DANGEROUS?**
☠ ☠ ☠ ☠ ☠

They hide in trees and spring with a deadly pounce

Leopards are the most **widespread** big cats, living across Africa and Asia. They **adapt** to many places, too, from **rocky hills** to thick forests, swamps, and even farmland. They **catch** a huge variety of **prey,** from beetles and mice, up to antelopes and even hippos!

**Killer fact**

A leopard can haul a kill twice its own weight up into tree branches, to feast in peace.

# Leopard

## Predator score

**Size up to:**
8 ft (2.4 m)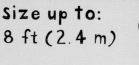

**Top speed:**
35 mph (56 km/h)

**HOW DANGEROUS?**

☠ ☠ ☠ ☠ ☠

It looks **weak** and floppy, but the box jellyfish is one of the **deadliest** creatures in the **world.** Its long tentacles have tiny stingers that inject extra-strong **venom** into any creature they touch. The tentacles then shorten to pull the **dying** victim up to its mouth on the underside of its main body.

Toxins in the tentacles attack the heart, nervous system, and skin cells

**Killer fact**

The jellyfish's venom is so powerful it can kill a human in less than four minutes.

# Box Jellyfish

**Predator score**

**Size up to:**
10 ft (3 m)

**Top speed:**
5 mph (8 km/h)

**HOW DANGEROUS?**

# Komodo Dragon

## Killer fact

The dragon's saliva (spit) is full of germs, so even if a bitten victim escapes, it dies of disease.

Poisonous spit hangs down from its mouth

The world's biggest lizard, the Komodo dragon has long claws, powerful jaws, and sharp teeth. It hunts living prey, like wild pigs or small deer, by thrashing them with its great tail. It also loves to chomp on the soft, smelly, rotten meat of dead animal bodies.

## Predator score

Size up to:
10 ft (3 m)

Top Speed:
11 mph (18 km/h)

HOW DANGEROUS?

☠ ☠ ☠ ☠ ☠

Some people are scared of their huge, hairy bodies and legs

**Killer fact**
Tarantulas flick hairs off their legs, which can blind small animals if they get into their eyes.

# Tarantula

Bigger than a human hand, the Mexican red-kneed tarantula is very strong, with a venomous bite.
It is sometimes called 'bird-eating spider', as it really does eat birds — as well as mice, rats, bats, lizards, snakes, bugs, worms, and even other spiders!

## Predator score

**Size up to:**
11 in (28 cm)

**Top Speed:**
18 mph (29 km/h)

**HOW DANGEROUS?**

# Lioness

Male lions roar and chase away other lion prides (groups), but the hunting is done by the female lions called lionesses. Some lionesses will **frighten** their victims, such as zebras or wildebeests, to make them run towards other lionesses who are hiding in the African grasslands. A deadly **ambush!**

Big jaws rip easily at flesh

## Killer fact

Lions can eat 60 lb (27 kg) of meat in one go – the same as a month of human meals!

## Predator score

**Size up to:**
8 ft (2.4 m)

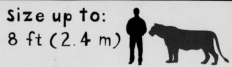

**Top Speed:**
50 mph (80 km/h)

**HOW DANGEROUS?**

# Leopard Seal

It has powerful jaws making it a fearsome predator

## Killer fact
The leopard seal can eat seven penguins in one day, although it usually leaves the feathers and beaks.

The leopard seal has spots, like the big cat of the same name — but the seal is twice the size, and hugely powerful. In the cold southern seas around Antarctica, this awesome killer makes lightning fast turns as it chases penguins, fish, squid, and even smaller seals.

## Predator score
**Size up to:**
11 ft (3.6 m)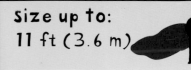

**Top speed:**
20 mph (32 km/h)

**HOW DANGEROUS?**

# Scorpion

Venom in the tail sting can paralyse prey

The scorpion sneaks around at night, looking for small prey like a bug, lizard, or mouse. It grabs the victim with its big pincers, injects in killer venom with its tail sting, and tears up the meal with its powerful cutting jaws.

**Killer fact**

In desert areas by day, scorpions look for a cool, dark place to hide, which could be someone's glove or shoe!

## Predator score

**Size up to:**
8 in (20 cm)

**Top speed:**
12 mph (19 km/h)

**HOW DANGEROUS?**
☠ ☠ ☠ ☠ ☠

Found in Africa and Asia, hyenas are famous scavengers — tearing skin and crunching bones left from the kills of other predators — but they are great hunters, too. A pack can bring down a hard-kicking zebra.

Tough, strong bodies mean they are able to pursue their prey to the death

## Hyena

### Killer fact
A hyena pack can eat a whole zebra in 30 minutes, including the bones, fur, and hooves!

## Predator score
**Size up to:**
5 ft (1.5 m)

**Top Speed:**
40 mph (64 km/h)

**HOW DANGEROUS?**
☠ ☠ ☠ ☠ ☠

With its front legs folded up as if ==praying,== the mantis is really preying — on any insect or other small creature that comes near. In a ==flash,== the mantis unfolds its ==spiky== front legs and **snaps** them shut on the meal, ==stabbing== in its spines. It then eats its victim while they are still ==alive.==

They are found widely in tropical regions

Spines for snaring and pinning prey in place

# Praying Mantis

**Predator score**

Size up to:
6 in (15 cm)

Top speed:
2 mph (3 km/h)

HOW DANGEROUS?
☠ ☠ ☠ ☠ ☠

# Snapping Turtle

They can stay submerged for 40 to 50 minutes before surfacing for air

## Killer fact

The little red flap in the turtle's mouth looks like a juicy worm to fish — one little nibble and snap!

This big, strong, North American turtle may lack **teeth**, but its mighty, sharp-edged jaws can **slice** a fish in half. The snapper likes to **catch** all kinds of food, such as frogs, snakes, birds, and even other **turtles!**

## Predator score

**Size up to:**
30 in (76 cm)

**Top Speed:**
2½ mph (4 km/h)

**HOW DANGEROUS?**

# Snowy owl

This owl's white feathers blend in with the ice and snow of northern lands, giving it perfect camouflage. Victims like lemmings, voles, and small birds hardly notice the owl until its sharp claws jab into them, and its hooked beak is tearing them apart.

**Killer fact**

They have a wingspan of 5 ft (1.5 m) making them powerful, fast flyers

## Predator score

**Size up to:**
2 ft (61 cm)

**Top Speed:**
50 mph (80 km/h)

# Glossary

**Accelerate** To pick up speed, going faster and faster.

**Camouflage** Where an animal's colour and pattern are similar to its surroundings, helping it to hide.

**Claw** A sharp nail on an animal's toe, used to stab, rip, tear, dig, or scratch.

**Fang** The long, sharp tooth of a creature such as a snake, fish or wolf. Some fangs inject venom into prey.

**Pack** A group of animals such as wolves or hyenas, who live and often hunt together.

■ A group of water animals such as whales or dolphins.

**Predator** An animal that hunts, kills and eats other creatures in order to survive.